THE GOD OF ABUNDANCE

AF722986

Mike Moore

The God of Abundance
by Mike Moore
©2020 Mike Moore
Printed in Canada
ISBN 978-1-7333716-1-2

All rights reserved solely by the author. The author guarantees all contents are original and do not infringe upon the legal rights of any other person or work. No part of this book may be reproduced, stored in a retrieval system, or transmitted in any form or by any means without expressed written permission of the author.

Printed by: Camden House Books, LLC
Contact: 918-361-6654
Edition: 4651-7

Editorial Director: Dr. Larry Keefauver www.doctorlarry.org Interior Design: Lisa Simpson www.simpsonproductions.net

Scriptures marked (KJV) are taken from the King James Version Public Domain.

Scriptures marked (NLT) are taken from the Holy Bible, New Living Translation, copyright © 1996, 2004, 2007, 2013, 2015 by Tyndale House Foundation. Used by permission of Tyndale House Publishers Inc., Carol Stream, Illinois 60188. All rights reserved.

Scriptures marked (AMP) are taken from the Amplified Bible Copyright © 2015 by The Lockman Foundation, La Habra, CA 90631. All rights reserved.

Scriptures marked (NIV) are taken from the Holy Bible, New International Version®, NIV® Copyright ©1973, 1978, 1984, 2011 by Biblica, Inc.® Used by permission. All rights reserved worldwide.

Scriptures marked (NKJV) are taken from the New King James Version®. Copyright © 1982 by Thomas Nelson. Used by permission. All rights reserved.

Scriptures marked (AMPC) are taken from the Amplified Bible, Classic Edition (AMPC) Copyright © 1954, 1958, 1962, 1964, 1965, 1987 by The Lockman Foundation.

Scriptures marked (NLV) are taken from the New Life Version copyright 1969, 2003 Barbour Publishing, Inc.

Table of Contents

INTRODUCTION
GOD'S WILL FOR YOUR LIFE IS ABUNDANCE

In John 10:10, Jesus says, "The thief cometh not, but for to steal, and to kill, and to destroy: I am come that they might have life, and that they might have it (life) more abundantly" (KJV emphasis added). Immediately, we realize an important truth that God is not our problem if we are not living an abundant life. Jesus explains that we have an enemy that He calls "the thief." We know that this enemy is the devil. Jesus warns us that the devil comes to steal our fellowship with God and our peace.

The enemy…

- wants to rob us of our health and to steal our joy and decimate our financial well-being.

- comes to kill our hopes and our ambitions.
- is at work to destroy our relationships so we are isolated and vulnerable to his attacks.
- seeks to torpedo the vision that God has placed in our hearts so that we are unable to move forward with God's plan for our lives.
- plans to undermine the God-ordained destiny of our lives so we cannot fulfill our mission in the Kingdom of God.

God's will is that every believer has more than enough resources to fulfill his or her personal God-given vision in life.

Jesus said, "I am come that you might have...." I always like to stop at the word "have." You see, God wants us to "have" something. He sent Jesus that we might "have life." The word "life" in this passage means fullness of life, a whole life—spiritually, mentally, emotionally, physically, socially, and financially. In fact, the Bible says in Ephesians 3:20, " Now to Him who is able to [carry out His purpose and] do **superabundantly** more than all that we dare ask or think [infinitely beyond our greatest prayers, hopes, or dreams], according to His power that is at work within us" (AMPC emphasis added).

The New Living Translation of John 10:10 says, "My purpose is to give them a rich and satisfying life." The Amplified Bible also expands on John 10:10 and says Jesus came that we might "have and enjoy life." Did you know it is possible to have something and not be satisfied and not enjoy it? It is possible to have a relationship and not enjoy that relationship or to have things and not enjoy those things.

For example, the people complained, grumbled, and murmured about everything as they journeyed out of Egypt and toward the Promised Land. Though they had an abundance of things and saw God's protection and provision, they were not satisfied and therefore could not enjoy the rich life God had planned for them. They even longed to go back into slavery.

The Amplified Bible says that Jesus came that we might have, enjoy, and have life more abundantly. Psalm 23:1 describes Jesus as our Shepherd and says, "The Lord is my Shepherd, I shall not lack" (AMPC). Lack means to be without that which is essential or needed like food, clothing, housing, transportation, job, and money to give for the work of the Kingdom.

Deuteronomy 8:9 says we will have "bread without scarcity" and "will lack nothing" (NKJV). Scarcity means having a very limited supply, barely enough, living a hand-to-mouth existence with no provision for emergencies, meeting the needs of others, or for unexpected expenses. In other words, there is nothing left over for savings.

Lack and poverty of body, soul, and spirit is not the life Jesus came to give us. It is God's will that we, His church, His children, are to have more than enough resources to establish His kingdom agendas and purposes as well as provide for all of our needs. Paul writes in Philippians 4:19, "and my God shall supply all your need according to His riches in glory by Christ Jesus" (NKJV).

When God instructed Moses to lead the people out of slavery and into their Promised Land, He made sure they would have more than enough to accomplish God's plan and purpose for them (Exodus 12:35-38 and 36:5-7).

Are You Fully Alive or Just Existing?

God is life; apart from Him there is not life only existence. Only people can live an abundant life. Animals exist, so do plants. People exist until they meet the Creator and the source of life—Jesus Christ.

Existence is holding on from day to day... just surviving.
  LIFE IN CHRIST is rejoicing daily in God's good plans.

Existence is dull and depressing.
  LIFE IN CHRIST is rejoicing always in His presence.

Existence longs for meaning and purpose.
LIFE IN CHRIST is presence-driven, purposeful productivity.

Existence is just enough.
LIFE IN CHRIST is more than enough.

May I ask you… are you ALIVE or just existing? The new life you experience in Jesus Christ is filled with abundance in the Spirit, in positive feelings and thoughts, and in physical provisions.

Life is abundance; existence is lack.
Life is plenty; existence is scarcity.
Life is success; existence is survival.

Consider the extravagance of God. The stars in the heavens and the particles of sand on a beach are innumerable. In a snowstorm, with the millions of snowflakes created, no two are alike. Every human being born is individually unique.

In this booklet, you will discover the amazing abundance that God through Christ has made available to you. Every single one of these words describes the life you ***have*** in Jesus Christ…if you decide to make Jesus Christ Lord and Savior of your life.

Prosperous
Plentiful
Abundant
Thriving
Copious
Affluent
Wealthy
Rich
Opulent
over the TOP!

Pause and Reflect…

Do you grumble and complain so much about the inconveniences of your life that you miss out on enjoying God's provision and protection?

Are you allowing the thief to come in and steal your fellowship with God and your peace, rob you of your health, and steal your joy and your financial well-being?

Have you allowed the enemy to kill your hopes and your ambitions and destroy your relationships?

Has this enemy attempted to destroy the vision that God has placed in your heart?

Are you ready to take back what the enemy has tried to kill, steal, and destroy in your life?

Are you tired of just making it, barely surviving, treading water and going nowhere?

When will you get tired of existing and start living the abundant life in Jesus Christ?

1

Abundance Defined

The word **abundance** Jesus used in describing the life He came to give us in John 10:10 has a two-fold meaning. One meaning is **superabundant in quantity**. Jesus demonstrated this to His disciples when He instructed them to put their boats out into the deep water and lower their nets for a haul. Though they had toiled all night and caught no fish, when they obeyed Jesus, they caught an abundance of fish, so much so that their nets were at the point of breaking (Luke 5:1-7).

Abundance here is defined as:

- to have more than necessary
- to exceed what is needed
- to have more than enough
- to have a surplus
- to go beyond measure
- to be excessive
- to overflow
- to have too much both corporately and individually

Jesus knew these men were businessmen and had families to support. They needed more than just enough. They needed an abundance.

In Exodus 36:5-7, it says, "And they spake unto Moses, saying, The people bring much more than enough (notice those words the people bring much more than enough) for the services of the work, which the Lord commanded to make. And Moses gave commandment, and they caused it to be proclaimed throughout the camp, saying, Let neither man nor woman make any more work for the offering of the sanctuary. So the people were restrained from bringing. For the stuff they had was sufficient for all the work to make it, and too much" (KJV emphasis added).

Notice it relates to our individual vision and it relates to our ministry in our local church which is a corporate vision. The Bible says the people brought much more than enough for the building of the tabernacle.

Hopefully, you have a dream, you have a goal, and you have something that you want to accomplish in life. It is going to take resources to accomplish that individual dream that you have.

Jesus came so that you might have too much… so you can accomplish your individual goals… and also help with the corporate goals… for the corporate vision of your local church body.

The other meaning of the word **abundance** is **superior in quality**. In the parable of the Prodigal Son in Luke 15:22-24, the prodigal went away, wasted his father's inheritance with riotous living, and ended up in the hog pen of life.

He repented, came to himself, and went back to his father. In verse 22, the father says, "bring forth the best" (KJV).

Your heavenly Father wants you to enjoy the best this life has to offer. That means God is not opposed to your personal comfort, convenience, or to have things to make the use of your time and energy more efficiently. For example, driving a car to your place of employment is probably more efficient than riding your bicycle, and traveling across the country is more efficient by plane than by car.

However, it is vitally important that believers understand why God wants them to have more than what they personally need.

God has a purpose for this abundance in our lives.

Pause and Reflect…

Do you have a dream, a goal, and something that you want to accomplish in life?

What resources will it take to accomplish that individual dream that you have?

2

God's Nature

His Name

To fully understand God's purpose for this abundance in a believer's life, we must first understand His nature. God's nature is first revealed to us through His name.

In Genesis 17:1, God appeared to Abram and said, "I am the Almighty God" (KJV). The English words, Almighty God, are translated in the Hebrew *El Shaddai* which means the All-Sufficient One. It means God is more than enough. His nature is evidenced and revealed first by His name, El Shaddai, the All-Sufficient One. He is the God that is more than enough.

Now, I want to caution you. Don't bring God down to the level of human experience, yours or others. We often make the mental mistake of evaluating who God is, His capacity, and His will for us by what's happening in our lives. Don't make the mistake of bringing God down to the level of your personal circumstances.

Let me explain. Personally and in ministry, I am blessed. At this point in my life, there is no struggle. At this point in my life, I am enjoying plenty. However, when God first began to reveal to me that He is the God of abundance, my wife and I were in a great struggle. We were living in a little starter two-bedroom house, with one bath and no furniture in the living room. I remember during the summer we were without air conditioning and my wife put aluminum foil in the windows to keep the house cool. I remember when we were looking between the seats of our car and our sofa trying to find money to go out and eat. That is when God showed me that He was a God of abundance. See, God is a God of abundance apart from human experience.

We have a blessed church. We have thousands of members; we have a full-time staff; we have over 2,000 volunteers; we have multiple campuses; we have 140 acres of land. Years ago, we completed a 16-million-dollar facility debt-free. Everything is paid for in my church, but in 1986, when God began to reveal to me that He was a God of abundance, we had less than 100 members. It took all the faith we could muster to believe God to get a loan for an abandoned school. The loan was only $25,000, but it took all the faith that we had to get that loan. The parking lot wasn't paved, the building needed renovation on the outside and on the inside, we had only old pews, screened doors, and no air conditioning. In that setting, God said, "I am a God of abundance." He is not the God of abundance because you enjoy abundance, and He is not the God of abundance because you are experiencing lack.

God is a God of abundance apart from our human experience.

The Law of Vision

There is a law in the Bible called the Law of Vision. It states that if you can't envision it, you can't have it. I want to stir up vision in you. In Genesis 13:14-15, the Bible says that after Lot was separated from Abram, God said to Abram: "Lift your eyes now and look from the place where you are—northward, southward, eastward, and westward; for all the land which you see," He said, "I am going to give it to you" (NKJV). Abram had to lift up his eyes from where he was to see what God was going to give him.

Pause and Reflect...

You've got to lift up your eyes from where you are:

What are you focusing on?

Are you focusing on your limitations and your weaknesses?

Are you focused on your circumstances, the economy, the government, your job, your business, your bank account, the prices at the gas pump?

What are you focusing on in your church, your membership roll?

What is God telling you to focus on?

Potential Is Measured by God Working with Us

Here's a statement that the Lord has been dealing with me about.

The measure of our potential is God working with us, through us, and for us.

Your potential is not determined or limited by your personal resources. Your potential is not determined or limited by your skill, your talent, your time, your money, your influence, or your education. Your potential as a church is not determined by or limited to your membership roll. It is not determined or limited by your bank statement. Your potential is measured by God working with you.

In Mark 16:20 it says, "The disciples went out and preached everywhere, and the Lord **worked with them** and confirmed his word by the signs that accompanied it" (NIV emphasis added).

Philippians 4:13 says, "I can do all things **through Christ** who strengthens me" (NKJV emphasis added).

Philippians 4:19 says, "but my God **shall supply all your need** according to

His riches in glory by Christ Jesus" (KJV emphasis added).

We fall short because we measure our potential by what we can do, what we can have, what we can become by our personal resources, and by our corporate resources. We never see the miracle hand of God because we won't move until we see the money in the bank. What we need more than money in the bank is a word from God because there is nothing that you can't accomplish with your faith. He is the God of abundance. His nature is revealed through His name. He is El Shaddai. He is the All-Sufficient One. He is the God that is more than enough.

Pause and Reflect...

Are you measuring your potential by what you can do, what you can have, what you can become by your personal resources?

Are you seeking more money in the bank more than you are seeking a word from God?

Poverty Is Not God's Will

Now notice in Deuteronomy 28:47-48, "Because thou servedst not the Lord thy God with joyfulness, and with gladness of heart, **for the abundance of all things**; Therefore shalt though serve thine enemies which the Lord shall send (or permit) against thee, in hunger, and in thirst, and in nakedness, and **in want of all things**: and he shall put a yoke of iron upon thy neck, until he have destroyed thee" (KJV emphasis added).

There are two things here in juxtaposition to each other. Verse 47 talks about "the abundance of all things." Verse 48 talks about "in want of all things." Let's look at verse 48 first. Verse 48 is a summary of the curse of disobedience. The words hunger, thirst, nakedness, and yoke of iron around the neck represent poverty.

Poverty is not God's will for your life.

Poverty manifests itself on three levels.

- **Level 1 Is Lack:** totally deficient, without that which is essential, without basic things, housing, clothing, food, shelter, transportation, money to give.
- **Level 2 Is Scarcity:** having a very limited supply, barely enough, no room for emergencies, no room for others, no room for savings. Scarcity is a hand-to-mouth existence.

Scarcity is living from payday to payday. The Lord said to me His "people are working every day and barely making it."

- **Level 3 Is Unfulfilled Desires:** This is not being able to enjoy godly desires. It is the inability to live beyond the need level.

Now, look at verse 47. It says, "the abundance of all things." Verse 47 is a summary of the blessing of obedience. Abundance is the will of God for your life.

Abundance is the will of God because His will has to be consistent with His nature. Dogs bark because barking is consistent with the nature of a dog. It is not God's will for you to have a little of anything because His nature is to bless us beyond what we think or imagine. In fact, it is impossible for God to give you a little of anything because it is inconsistent with His nature. It is impossible for me to give birth to a child. Giving birth to a baby, being a male, is inconsistent with my nature. It is inconsistent with the nature of God to give you a little.

If you have a little and only have enough, it is not because God gave you a little and it is not because God gave you just enough. His will has to be consistent with His nature and God's nature is revealed through His name, El Shaddai, the All-Sufficient One, the God that is more than enough.

Pause and Reflect...

Are you experiencing lack, scarcity or unfulfilled godly desires in your life?

Are you tired of living a life of poverty?

Are you serving God with joyfulness and with gladness of heart?

If not, repent so you can move forward into the abundance of all things.

God's Vocabulary

God's nature is evidenced by His name, but God's nature is also evidenced by His vocabulary. You can learn a lot about a person by listening to the words that come out of their mouths. If you want to know what a person thinks or what a person feels about a matter, pay attention to their conversation. The Scripture says, "Out of the abundance of the heart, the mouth speaks" (Matthew 12:34 NKJV).

Would you agree that the Bible is God speaking to us? Therefore, out of the abundance of His heart, He is speaking through His written Word. This means we can know what He thinks, what He feels, and His thoughts on a matter by what He says in His Word. I studied this out and discovered God's speech is filled with superlatives. When He uses adjectives and adverbs to express Himself concerning what is in His heart, He always uses the extreme, highest, maximum, supreme form or degree. Sometimes we read Scriptures, but we don't meditate on them enough to get what is really going on. I'll give you some illustrations.

Psalm 23:5 says, "Thou preparest a table before me in the presence of mine enemies: thou anointest my head with oil; my cup runneth over" (KJV). Now, what causes a thing to run over? It's too much.

Malachi 3:10 says, "Bring ye all the tithes into the storehouse, that there may be meat in mine house, and prove me now herewith, saith the Lord of hosts, if I will not open you the windows of heaven, and pour you out a blessing, that there shall not be room enough to receive it" (KJV). Not room enough to receive implies that there is too much.

Then Luke 6:38 says, "Give, and it shall be given unto you; good measure, pressed down, and shaken together, and running over, shall men give into your bosom" (KJV). Again, we see the phrase, "running over."

Your potential is not determined by or limited by your personal or corporate resources. Your potential is measured by God working with you, through you, and for you. Ephesians 3:20 says, "Now unto him that is able to do (now notice the superlatives) **exceeding abundantly** above all that we ask or think, according to the power that worketh in us" (KJV emphasis added). That power working in us is the faith to believe He can and will do exceedingly abundantly above all we ask or think.

Pause and Reflect...

> *What did you discover about God's nature through His vocabulary?*
>
> *How does your vocabulary reveal your faith to believe God can and will do exceedingly abundantly above all you ask or think?*
>
> *Do your words speak abundance or poverty?*
>
> *Do your words speak more than enough or scarcity?*
>
> *Do your words speak running over or lack?*

3

God Is Not Wasteful

Does Psalm 68:19 say, "Blessed be the Lord, who daily loadeth us with problems, cares, trouble, pain?" No, it says, "Who daily loadeth us with benefits" (KJV). What is a benefit? It is something that promotes well-being and adds to life. A benefit is something good. Notice, He doesn't just give us benefits, He loads us with benefits.

The word **load** means:

- to fill to overflowing
- to pile
- to fill to excess by compressing or squeezing tightly
- to cram
- to supply in abundance or excess

Psalm 68:19 says God **daily** loads us with benefits. However, many Christians will live and die in yesterday's blessings. If we would keep our faith engaged, then we can receive from God every day.

In Matthew 21:21, Jesus told His disciples, "I tell you the truth, if you have faith and don't doubt, you can do things like this and much more. You can even say to this mountain, 'May you be lifted up and thrown into the sea,' and it will happen" (NLT). God blessed us yesterday, but why can't He bless us today? There are two qualifying issues that we have to look at. Number one, we have to look at the issue of stewardship. Secondly, we have to look at the issue of purpose, understanding the purpose for the excess.

Stewardship

So, let's talk about stewardship for just a moment. The Bible says that a certain man had three servants. (The man represented the Lord in the story.) He was planning to go into a far-off country and he called his servants in and he delivered his goods to them. To one he gave five talents, to the second he gave two talents, and to the third he gave one talent. The five-talent man went out, gained five talents more, and the man commended his servant saying, "Well done." The two-talent man went out, gained two more talents, and the Lord commended him as well. The one-talent man buried the talent and was reprimanded by the Lord (see Matthew 25:14-27).

Then, there is an interesting thing that I noticed in verses 28 and 29. After reprimanding the unfaithful servant, the Lord said to take from him the one talent and give it to him that has ten. That seems unfair because he already had ten. Then the Lord says, "every one that hath shall be given more." Now, notice what it says is "he shall have abundance." Two things I want you to notice from this because this issue of stewardship is one of the things that is going to qualify us for abundance.

God does not give more to bad stewards, whether it be the stewardship of our tithes, our talents, or our financial resources.

This is a critical issue. We lack discernment in this area of giving in our individual lives and in our churches. There are some people who have legitimate needs caused by factors outside of their control. There are also some people in a state of need because of their own disobedience or irresponsibility and are poor stewards. God does not give more to bad stewards. Do you?

Are you praying for more? Are you a good steward of what you already have? Why should God give you more if you are wasting what you already have? If you're taking God's resources and giving to others who are irresponsible, those who are disobedient, then you are giving money to folks you shouldn't give money to. You are believing God for more, but God doesn't give more to bad stewards. If you are not discerning in your giving individually then you could end up wasting resources and God will not give you any more because you are not responsible with what you have.

Even in our churches, there are people who refuse to tithe. It is not an issue of ignorance, it's an issue of "I'm not going to tithe." So, is it good stewardship for pastors to take tithes and offerings that came from givers to give to folks who are bad stewards? I found myself making this mistake early in my ministry. I was praying for more, "Lord, give me more members. Lord, give me more leaders. Lord, give me more workers. Lord, give me more money." Oftentimes, we are looking outside of ourselves when the critical issue is what are we doing with the members we have, the leaders we have, and the money we have? Are we good stewards? God doesn't give more to bad stewards.

He does give more to good stewards. That's why there are times when God will move on you to give to someone who already has something. There are times when God will move on your heart to give to someone who has plenty because the reason they may have plenty is because they were good stewards. God wants them to have more because a good steward recognizes that he is a steward of what God has given him.

Stewardship is an essential and critical issue if we are going to experience abundance.

Purpose

Now the second issue is purpose. Jesus came so that we might have too much, but to qualify, we must understand the purpose for the excess.

Jesus went up into the mountain, sat down with His disciples, lifted up His eyes, and saw a crowd coming. Jesus turned to Philip and said, "Where can we buy bread, so these may eat?" The Scripture says He knew what He would do, but Philip didn't understand that his potential was not determined by the personal and corporate resources he had available. Philip scanned the crowd and said, "Two hundred pennyworths is not enough to give them a little." His words proved that he had a "little bit" mentality. Then, Andrew spoke up, "There is a little lad here that has five loaves and two fish, but what are they among so many?" Jesus said, "Give me what you've got" (see John 6:3-9).

Jesus did three things when He received the five loaves and two fish. If you read Matthew, Mark, and John's accounts, the Bible says the first thing He did was to give thanks. He thanked God for what He had. See, you've got to begin there, thanking God for what you have. Jesus looked up from the "not enough" to God who is "more than enough." Then, secondly, He blessed it. See, you've got to start saying the right thing. He thanked God, He looked up, then He spoke the right things. Thirdly, He began to distribute the food to the disciples. The Bible says that the folks ate as much as they wanted. John 6:12 says and when they were filled, Jesus said, "Gather up the fragments that remain, so that nothing be lost" (NKJV).

God is extravagant but He is not wasteful. There were twelve baskets over and above what was needed for each person to receive until they were filled. The thing I thought about with this is surely God knew how much it would have taken to feed these folks and not have anything left over. But the Bible says that there were twelve baskets over and above what the 5,000 ate.

God had a purpose for the excess. The excess was not for those who had eaten because the Bible says they ate until they were filled and then they were dismissed. So, the excess must have been for somebody else. Some folks say it was for the little lad who gave Jesus his lunch. It could have been for the twelve disciples because there were twelve baskets. We don't know, but God had a purpose for the excess because Jesus told His disciples,

"Gather up now the fragments (the broken pieces that are left over), so that **nothing may be lost and wasted**" (John 6:12 AMPC emphasis added).

Notice, if Jesus had not allowed the excess to come, God's purpose for the excess would not have been fulfilled. What if Jesus had said, "They have enough, cut the miracle off," then God's purpose for the excess would not have been fulfilled.

2 Corinthians 9:8 says, "And God is able to make all grace abound toward you; that ye, always having all sufficiency in all things, may abound to every good work" (KJV). You will notice that the word "abound" means abundance and excess. Also, notice that the word "abound" is mentioned twice. First, so that you always having all sufficiency in all things (that's a first-class lifestyle). However, it did not

stop there. It goes on to say, that you may abound to every good work.

God's purpose for excess, for His blessings to abound in your life, is so that you can abound in every good work. It is critical that you realize this and be a good steward with all that God has given you.

Pause and Reflect…

Would God describe you as a good steward over what He has given you?

Have you handled any excess blessings in your life to abound in every good work?

How has the warning in this lesson inspired you to be a better steward of all that God has given you?

4

Mindsets that Rob Believers

> *For as he thinketh in his heart so is he.* (Proverbs 23:7 KJV)

Instead of having an abundant life mentality, believers may develop mindsets that will rob them of what Jesus came to give them as stated in John 10:10. These negative mindsets allow the thief to come in to kill, steal, and destroy the life God wants for every believer.

- **Fatalistic Mentality**: I have no power to influence my future. It is what it is. What is going to happen cannot be changed. This must be the life God wants me to have and there is nothing I can do to change it (see Jeremiah 13:23).
- **Victim Mentality:** I am the victim of the negative actions of others (see Genesis 3:9-12).
- **Complacent Mentality**: I am satisfied with how things are, I have need of nothing more (see Revelation 3:17).
- **Constraint Mentality**: I am limited by my beliefs, abilities, and resources (see Luke 5:4-6, Psalm 78:41).

A failure to understand the purpose for the abundance is a major reason many believer's prayers go unanswered. The Bible says in James 4, you have not because you ask not. You ask and you receive not because you are asking amiss.

Another mindset that robs believers is what many Christians think is humility. See, if you only want just enough in life and are not interested in learning about abundance, you are asking amiss. That's not humility, that's selfishness. If you only have just enough, you can't help anyone else. Nobody said you had to keep the excess. In fact, we are called to use our talents, energy, and the excess God gives us to help the poor, widows, orphans, and homeless.

God needs you to believe for the excess because He has a purpose for the excess. The reason some of us are not getting our prayers answered is because we are only asking for just enough. We need to understand the purpose for the excess, the purpose for the abundance. If we don't understand the purpose, we don't qualify for abundance.

Pause and Reflect...

Review the mindsets listed above and see if you need to deal with one or more of them so you can begin to receive the abundance God has for you.

What purpose has God revealed to you for the excess He gives you?

Quality, Quantity, and Capacity

1 Timothy 6:17 says, "As for the rich in this present world, instruct them not to be conceited *and* arrogant, nor to set their hope on the uncertainty of riches,

but on God, **who richly *and* ceaselessly provides** us with everything for our enjoyment" (AMP emphasis added). The word richly there means abundantly, copiously, lavishly. That's describing a first-class lifestyle.

God doesn't just give us all things to enjoy, though. We can't stop there because if we stop there, we won't understand the purpose for the excess. 1 Timothy 6:18 says, "Tell them to use their money to do good. They should be rich in good works and generous to those in need, always being ready to share with others" (NLT). There are three things that he mentions there: the quality, quantity, and the capacity to perform.

Quality means excellence. It takes resources to do things with excellence. Excellence costs more, but you are better off in the long run. If we are going to win the lost, we are going to have to operate in excellence.

This is a problem I see in the church. I believe God is not going to give us a whole lot of money if we don't straighten this out. When it comes to ministering to the needy, we are always giving them stuff we don't want. What do I mean by that? We are always giving the needy second-hand, worn out, thrift-shop items. Even our food pantries are filled with junk. Scripture says that they are to use their money to do **good works**. That's the **quality** of the works. When we are helping folks, we should do it with **quality**. In our churches, if we are going to reach out to people, and we're going to have programs and ministries, we should do it with quality, but excellence costs more. One of God's purposes for giving us abundance, for giving us excess and more than enough is for us to use it to do good works.

He said they are also to be **rich** in good works and give generously. That's the **quantity** of the works. Only the rich can be rich in good works and give generously. That's why it said charge them that are rich in this world to do these good works. If you have more, you can do more. However, we need to realize greed is not wanting more money. There is nothing wrong with wanting more money. In fact, something is wrong with you if you don't want more money. Greed is not wanting more money. Greed is wanting more money for self only.

They are also to always be ready and willing to share with others. That is the **capacity to perform**. He says they are to be willing. That has to do with our attitude. We've got to want to. Then he says they are to be ready. That is having resources in hand. We can be willing and not be ready.

I was willing to do things for folks years ago, but I wasn't ready. If you don't have any resources in hand, you may be willing, but you are not ready. You have to have the capacity to perform. It's willingness and then you have to be ready.

In 1 Timothy 6:19, the Apostle Paul explains how to be ready. "Laying up in store for themselves a good foundation against the time to come, that they may lay hold on eternal life" (KJV). Number one is **laying up in store for themselves**. The Amplified translation says, "storing up for themselves the *enduring* riches." How do we store up enduring riches for ourselves? The Scripture teaches that we provide for ourselves through our giving. Now that's a paradox, but the way we provide for ourselves is not by holding on to what we have been given. The way we provide for ourselves is by giving. Jesus said in Luke 12:33, "Give alms; provide yourselves bags which wax not old, a treasure in the heavens that faileth not, where no thief approacheth, neither moth corrupteth" (KJV). So, the Bible teaches that the way we provide for ourselves and the way we establish enduring riches, a heavenly banking account that will not fail us regardless of the economic conditions, regardless of the gas prices, regardless of what's going on with mortgage prices and interest rates is through our giving.

Notice the second thing he says is laying **a good foundation**. The New Life Version says, "Then they will be gathering together riches for themselves. These good things are what they will build on for the future. Then they will have the only true life!"

Building on a good foundation is essential for achieving the only true life. A good foundation is achieved through obedience. In Luke 6:46-48, Jesus said, "But why do you call Me 'Lord, Lord,' and not do the things which I say? Whoever comes to Me, and hears My sayings and does them, I will show you whom he is like: He is like a man building a house, who dug deep and laid the foundation on the rock. And when the flood arose, the stream beat vehemently against that house, and could not shake it, for it was founded on the rock" (NKJV). Now watch this, "But he who heard and did nothing is like a man who built a house on the earth without a foundation, against which the stream beat vehemently; and immediately it fell. And the ruin of that house was great" (verse 49 NKJV).

So, the necessary good foundation for abundance is built on obedience to God's Word and His principles.

We are in a time now where we are going to have to obey the written Word, but we are going to have to also obey the voice of the Lord in our spirit. It's our obedience that is the good foundation. He says, laying up in store for yourselves a good foundation against the time to come.

Pause and Reflect...

It is vitally important that we understand the importance of what the Apostle Paul wrote in 1 Timothy 6:17-19. If we do not grasp these important concepts about the abundant life, we will not be prepared for the time to come.

Scripture says that they do good works. What does this mean?

How does it say we are to provide for ourselves, others, and establish a heavenly banking account that will not fail us regardless of the economic conditions, regardless of the gas prices, regardless of what's going on with mortgage prices and interest rates?

How do we lay a good foundation so we can be ready for what is to come?

5

The Believer's Responsibility

What is responsibility? It is something we are required to do, an obligation. It is obediently taking action according to God's instructions. We are the ones laying that good foundation. We are the ones called to do the good works. God will provide what we need and abundantly when we obediently act on what He tells us to do.

When Peter and his fellow fishermen were instructed by Jesus to take their boat out again after not catching any fish all night long and lower their nets where Jesus told them to, they were responsible to follow those instructions. When they did, they received an abundance of fish.

When the disciples followed Jesus' instructions to wait in Jerusalem for the Holy Spirit, they received the power to reach people from all nations for the Lord.

When they then went out and followed the instructions Jesus gave them in the Great Commission, the Lord worked with them and confirmed His word with signs.

Jesus said in Luke 12:48, "For everyone to whom much is given, from him much will be required" (NKJV). God will provide abundantly for those who are willing to take action and obediently use what He has given.

We determine how much we receive from God. His abundance is limitless. What limits abundance is our self-imposed, finite capacity to believe and receive.

The Widow's Oil

In 2 Kings 4:1-7, we read the account of the widow's oil. First of all, she took the initiative and went to the prophet Elisha and explained the situation. Her husband, who had revered the Lord, had died and his creditor was now coming after his widow and threatening to take her two sons as slaves to repay her husband's debt.

Elisha asked the widow two questions: How can I help you? What do you have in your house? In other words, she was going to have to use what she already had. Elisha would help her, but he was not going to do it for her.

Elisha told her to go around to her neighbors and ask for empty jars, and not just a few. The woman had to go and do what the prophet of the Lord instructed her to do. She had to take some action. She was not just to sit on her front porch and wait for God or the prophet to do everything for her. Now, Elisha did not specify how many empty jars she was to ask for, but he said not just a few. At some point, she and her sons decided they had enough empty vessels.

Even though she did not understand what was going to happen, she trusted God and followed the prophet's instructions. He told her what to do and she and her sons obeyed.

In verse 6, they ran out of empty jars and then the oil stopped. God did not run out of oil, they ran out of empty jars.

When she told Elisha what had happened, he told her to sell the oil and pay her debts. Then they were to live on what was left. God supplied more than enough to meet their needs as well as pay their debts.

The widow's responsibility was to obey the Lord. When she did, her family was saved from ruin.

What Is Our Responsibility?

Our commitment is to obey the Holy Spirit's instructions.

Our capacity is to believe in God's ability to meet our needs above and beyond what we can even imagine.

Our hearts are to be open to receive the abundant life our heavenly Father desires for us.

Responsibility = Responding to God's Ability to Provide

And God is able to make all grace [every favor and earthly blessing] come in abundance to you, so that you may always [under all circumstances, regardless of the need] have complete sufficiency in everything [being completely self-sufficient in Him], and have an abundance for every good work and act of charity. (2 Corinthians 9:8 AMP)

And God will generously provide all you need. Then you will always have everything you need and plenty left over to share with others. (2 Corinthians 9:8 NLT)

GOD IS ABLE IS THE MASTER KEY TO "TOO MUCH."

Pause and Reflect...

What instructions have you received from God?

What is your responsibility?

Remember, God is not limited. You determine how much you receive from God.

Final Word

Real Life

In 1 Timothy 6:19, the Apostle Paul explains the reason we are to be ready. "Laying up in store for themselves a good foundation **against the time to come,** that they may lay hold on eternal life" (KJV emphasis added).

In Exodus 10:22, the Bible says that Moses stretched his hand toward heaven and great darkness came over Egypt. The

Bible says for three days the Egyptians could not see one another neither did they move from their place. But all Israel had light in their dwellings. I believe that is where we are headed in the "time to come."

The Spirit of the Lord spoke to me on October 2, 2000, and said economic upheaval is coming. Then He said to me on November 11, 2004, provision is coming. I call it the great paradox. At the same time where there is great economic upheaval, there will be great provision. At the same time that there was darkness in Egypt, there was light in Israel. I'm telling you, economic upheaval is coming, but great provision is also coming.

1 Timothy 6:19 says, "Laying up in store for themselves a good foundation against the time to come, **that they may lay hold on eternal life**" (KJV emphasis

added). Laying up in store for themselves a good foundation through obedience will prepare us against the time to come so that we may lay hold on eternal life. How can a Christian lay hold on eternal life? Aren't we saved now?

The New Life Version says, "Then they will be gathering together riches for themselves. These good things are what they will build on for the future. **Then they will have the only true life!**"

The phrase "eternal life" there is not talking about being born again. It's what's real life. That's what eternal life in this context means. You will lay hold on real living. See, real living is verses 17 and 18. Real living is being richly supplied so you can enjoy all things, but if you stop right there you haven't laid hold to what real life is all about.

That's what the rich young ruler's problem was in Mark 10:17-20. He was already wealthy. He came to Jesus and asked, "What must I do to inherit eternal life?" Jesus did not say you must be born again. Jesus said, "You know the commandments." The rich young ruler said, "I've done those."

Now listen, this rich young ruler was enjoying life, but that's not real living. To just sit up on the hill and live a first-class lifestyle, that's not real living. You haven't really lived until you do good works, be rich in good works, ready to share, and willing to give generously. That was his shortage. He knew something was missing. He had all these material things, but he knew something was missing.

In verse 21, Jesus said, "One thing you lack, go and give." In other words, he needed to have the whole package. He needed to understand God's purpose for the excess.

God wants us to enjoy this life and be richly blessed, but we can't stop at being blessed. God needs us to release our faith for the abundance because He's got a purpose for the excess. If we can get the church to release their faith for the abundance, then God's purpose for the excess will be fulfilled.

Pause and Reflect…

Do you feel something is missing in your life?

What did you learn to help you begin to live the real life Jesus came to provide for you?

ABOUT THE AUTHOR

Mike Moore is the founder and president of Mike Moore Ministries and author of numerous books including the popular "***Weep Not: Overcoming Grief, Disappointment, and Loss***" and "***Moving from Tragedy to Triumph.***" He built this global ministry decades ago upon the simple yet profound truth that "The Word of God is the Answer" for every situation. His easy-to-follow messages provide practical ways to apply God's Word to every day, real life circumstances.

He is the Senior Pastor of Faith Chapel. In addition to providing spiritual mentorship to an alliance of pastors, Moore can be seen on his ***Answers That Work*** television broadcast, YouTube channel, ***How To Win*** podcast, and at conferences.

He is married to Kennetha and they have two adult children, Michael and Tiffany.

ABOUT MIKE MOORE MINISTRIES

Mike Moore Ministries, a global ministry founded by Mike Moore, was built upon the simple yet profound truth that "The Word of God is the Answer" to all of life's questions. Through various mediums which include television, digital, and print, Moore teaches that God wants His people to live a prosperous life — a prosperity that exceeds the boundaries of just finances. This prosperity encompasses spiritual prosperity, physical health, relationships, mental health, and financial independence.

Additional resources from Mike Moore
can be obtained by visiting
mikemooreministries.org or by calling
toll free **1-866-930-WORD (9673).**

MIKE MOORE
MINISTRIES
MIKEMOOREMINISTRIES.ORG